TALES of MADISON FAITH

D0772007

Yummy Yummy Nummy Nummy,
should I put this in my tummy?

By Kim MacGregor

Illustrated by Sharon Snider and Todd Remy

For Jeff and Maddie who make my world delicious - KM

" I am delighted that a portion of the proceeds from this wonderful series of storybooks will be donated to the Canadian Cystic Fibrosis Foundation. Kim MacGregor and I have two things in common; we are both mothers, and cystic fibrosis has touched both of our families. I lost my beloved niece Karine to CF in 1993. I have long been a supporter of the Canadian Cystic Fibrosis Foundation and its efforts to find a cure for this devastating disease. Kim's contribution to this effort is truly admirable."

Céline Dion,
Celebrity Patron of the
Canadian Cystic Fibrosis Foundation

Text copyright © 2002 by Kim MacGregor
Illustrations copyright © 2002 by Sharon Snider and Todd Reny
All rights reserved.
No part of this work covered by the copyrights heron may be reproduced
or used in any form or by any means - graphic, electronic, or mechanical - without the prior
written permission of the publisher.
Published in Canada by Beautiful Beginnings Youth Inc.
60-8 Bristol Road East, Suite 102 Mississauga, Ontario L4Z 3K8

National Library of Canada Cataloguing in Publication

MacGregor, Kim, 1968-
    Yummy yummy nummy nummy, should I put this in my tummy?/
by Kim MacGregor ; illustrated by Sharon Snider and Todd Reny.

(Tales of Madison Faith) Poems. For children.
ISBN 0-9731301-0-5 (bound).—ISBN 0-9731301-2-1 (pbk.)

1. Food--Juvenile poetry. 2. Children's poetry, Canadian (English) I. Snider, Sharon, 1951-
III. Reny, Todd, 1972- IV. Title. V. Series: MacGregor, Kim, 1968- Tales of Madison Faith.

PS8575.G825Y85 2002   jC811'.6   C2002-903432-9
PZ8.3.M15925Yu 2002

Printed and bound in Hong Kong, China by Book Art Inc., Toronto

Other Tales of Madison Faith Books:
"Button, Buckle, Tie"
To find out more about Madison Faith visit us at:
www.talesofmadisonfaith.com
Email us at: macgregor3@idirect.com

1 2 3 4 5 6   07 06 05 04 03

I love to crawl around the floor

it is so yummy to explore.

I find a tasty, 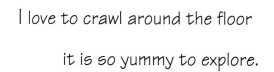 treat

and pop it in
my mouth to eat.

I swish it left then swish it right

that's when I see

my mommy's fright.

She runs to me.
I hear her shout!

"Madison Faith,
now spit that out!"

I open up and let it drop
it lands in mommy's hand *kerflop.*

"You can't eat
everything you see,
especially not this
yellow key!"

It sparkled bright and caught my eye.

But can't I eat it? Why-oh-why?

I do not want to spit it out.

What is this spitting thing about?

I need your help! Please let me know -

if I can't eat it,

just yell NO !

Something **brown** just caught my eye,

here I go to have a try.

I've seen these things around Dad's feet.

I'll bet these laces will taste sweet.

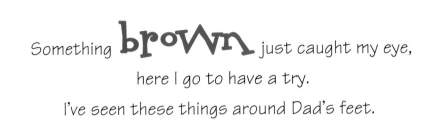

should I put
shoes in my
tummy?

NO!

Something **red**
just caught my eye,
here I go to have a try.
It's small and round with polka dots-
first I'll lick those tiny spots.

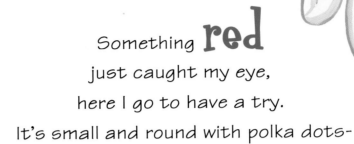

**Yummy Yummy
Nummy Nummy,**

should I put
bugs in my tummy?

NO!

Something Orange just caught my eye,
here I go to have a try.
Mommy wears this on her head,
but I will crunch it up instead.

Yummy Yummy
Nummy Nummy,

should I put

hats in my

tummy?

Something **blue** just caught my eye,

here I go to have a try.

It bounces up and down the town,

I'll chomp it up and swallow it down.

Yummy Yummy Nummy Nummy,

should I put **balls** in my tummy?

Something **white** just caught my eye,
here I go to have a try.
Mom holds this to her ear and talks.
I'll eat it while I try to walk.

**Yummy Yummy
Nummy Nummy,**

should I
put **phones**
in my tummy?

Something **green** just caught my eye,
here I go to have a try.
Nibbling this would be such fun.
It goes much faster than I run.

Yummy Yummy Nummy Nummy,

should I
put **cars**
in my tummy?

NO!

You have said **No** to everything.
What can I eat?

What is **Okay?**

I'd like to

eat
something
today!

Mmmmmmmm...

Some mixed up colors just caught my eye,

here I go to have a try.

There's grape juice, pizza topped with cheese,

ice cream sundaes, corn and peas.

Yummy Yummy Nummy Nummy,

should I put

food in my

tummy?

Ha ha! Hee hee! Now I can see,
it's food that is so good for me.

When I eat food, mommy won't shout:

"Madison Faith, now spit that out!"

Yummy Yummy
Nummy Nummy,

I have a great **big**
filled up tummy?